BASKETBALL

WHO DOES WHAT?

BY RYAN NAGELHOUT

Gareth Stevens
PUBLISHING

Please visit our website, www.garethstevens.com. For a free color catalog of all our high-quality books, call toll free 1-800-542-2595 or fax 1-877-542-2596.

Cataloging-in-Publication Data

Names: Nagelhout, Ryan.
Title: Basketball: who does what? / Ryan Nagelhout.
Description: New York : Gareth Stevens Publishing, 2018. | Series: Sports: what's your position? | Includes index.
Identifiers: ISBN 9781538205198 (pbk.) | ISBN 9781538204221 (library bound) | ISBN 9781538204283 (6 pack)
Subjects: LCSH: Basketball–Juvenile literature.
Classification: LCC GV885.1 N34 2018 | DDC 796.323–dc23

First Edition

Published in 2018 by
Gareth Stevens Publishing
111 East 14th Street, Suite 349
New York, NY 10003

Copyright © 2018 Gareth Stevens Publishing

Designer: Sarah Liddell
Editor: Ryan Nagelhout

Photo credits: Cover, p. 1 Monkey Business Images/Shuttestock.com; jersey texture used throughout Al Sermeno Photography/Shutterstock.com; chalkboard texture used throughout Maridav/Shutterstock.com; pp. 5, 10, 13, 15, 21 Aspen Photo/Shutterstock.com; p. 6 JAVIER SORIANO/Staff/AFP/Getty Images; p. 7 Eyes wide/Shutterstock.com; p. 9 Jason Miller/Stringer/Getty Images Sport/Getty Images; p. 11 Kittichai/Shutterstock.com; p. 17 Focus On Sport/Contributor/Getty Images Sport/Getty Images; p. 19 Tom Pidgeon/Stringer/Getty Images Sport/Getty Images; p. 22 Ronald Martinez/Staff/Getty Images Sport/Getty Images; p. 23 Brett Carlsen/Contributor/Getty Images Sport/Getty Images; p. 25 Icon Sports Wire/Contributor/Icon Sportswire/Getty Images; p. 27 Gregory Shamus/Staff/Getty Images Sport/Getty Images; p. 28 Thearon W. Henderson/Getty Images Sport/Getty Images; p. 29 The Washington Post/Contributor/The Washington Post/Getty Images.

Printed in the United States of America

CPSIA compliance information: Batch #CS17GS: For further information contact Gareth Stevens, New York, New York at 1-800-542-2595.

CONTENTS

Words in the glossary appear in **bold** type the first time they are used in the text.

CHANGING POSITIONS

Whether cutting a hole in the bottom of the basket or adding the three-point line, few sports have changed over the years as much as basketball. And that includes the positions people play on the court. There are only a few basic kinds of player, but they often fill many different positions on a team.

What's more, teams can play different groups of players on the court at any time. That means many different groups of players can be on the basketball court at any time. So let's check in and see what we can learn about the positions in basketball!

50 PLAYERS PER TEAM?

In the first rules for basketball, there was no limit to the number of players a team could have on the court. Some games even had 50 people on each team! The game has changed a lot since then. Today, the rules are simple: five players per team at all times.

4

COULD YOU IMAGINE WATCHING 100 PEOPLE TRY TO PLAY BASKETBALL ON THE SAME COURT? TEN PLAYERS PER GAME IS ENOUGH TODAY!

THE STARTING FIVE

There are five basic positions in basketball. Players often occupy set spots on the court when they're trying to run plays and score points. The basic positions are divided between two different areas—the frontcourt and the backcourt.

The frontcourt includes the players that usually play closest to the net. These are called forwards. The post player, or center, plays right near the net. The power forward usually plays to the left of the net, and the small forward plays to the right. The backcourt is made up of guards—usually a point guard and a shooting guard.

So how do you pick a position in basketball? The best way is to try them all out for yourself. Learning to shoot hoops with your friends is often best to figure out how you like to play. Knowing what you're best at will help you decide where on the floor you should play.

HERE ARE THE FIVE BASIC POSITIONS ON A BASKETBALL TEAM. WHICH WOULD YOU LIKE TO PLAY?

THE STARTING FIVE

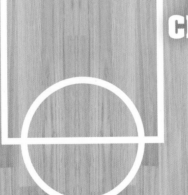

5 CENTER

4 POWER FORWARD

3 SMALL FORWARD

2 SHOOTING GUARD

1 POINT GUARD

Point guard is often thought of as the most important position in basketball. Point guards are like the quarterback of a basketball team. They run scoring plays on offense and make a lot of passes to teammates spread out on the floor. Point guards are named after where they often play from—the point, or the top of the key painted on the floor.

Whether they're passing or shooting, point guards need to be fast and smart so they can make quick plays. If they see an opening, point guards will drive toward the net to shoot. Other times, they'll pass to other players, then stay in the backcourt and be ready to get back on defense.

SHORT STUFF?

Point guards are often the shortest players on the team, but not always. Giannis Antetokounmpo (YAHN-ihs ah-deh-toh-KOON-boh) is a 6-foot-11-inch (2.1 m) player for the Milwaukee Bucks. He's known for his amazing dunks, but the "Greek Freak" often plays point guard for the Bucks! If you have the skills to play point, it doesn't matter how tall you are.

GIANNIS
ANTETOKOUNMPO

SHOOTERS SHOOT

A shooting guard's job is pretty easy to guess. They're often the best shooter on the team, which means they're able to score all over the court. Shooting guards play to the left of a point guard and must always be ready to shoot. Their quick, **accurate** shots are worth three points if they shoot them behind the three-point arc on the floor out past the key.

Point guards usually have better ball-handling skills than shooting guards, but both need to be good at **dribbling** and moving around defenders. Shooting guards need to get to spots on the floor they know they can make shots from.

Offensive plays are often **designed** to get the ball to the shooting guard. They need to move quickly to get to certain spots on the floor to take passes from the point guard. Sometimes, they'll get help from a teammate to get open.

SHOOTING GUARDS PRACTICE SHOOTING FROM ALL OVER THE FLOOR. THEY NEED TO MAKE BIG SHOTS WHEN THEY GET PASSED THE BALL.

THE BASKETBALL COURT

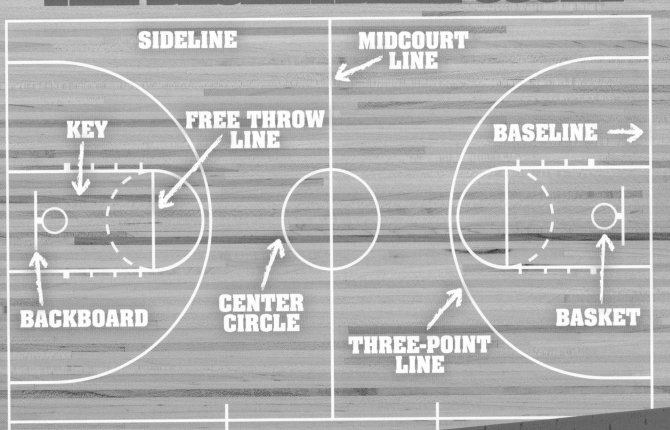

SIDELINE

MIDCOURT LINE

KEY

FREE THROW LINE

BASELINE →

BACKBOARD

CENTER CIRCLE

THREE-POINT LINE

BASKET

Small forwards aren't often very small compared to guards! They're called the "three" in basketball. Small forwards are usually the best all-around player on the team. They can play both close to and away from the net. Small forwards usually play on the right side of the court. They're usually taller and stronger than the guards.

Small forwards need to shoot, but they also need to use their size to track down shots they or another player missed. This is called rebounding. When an offense gets a rebound, they have another chance to score points.

TOOLS OF THE JOB

Small forwards aren't always shorter than the other forwards, but they usually have skills these players lack. They often have less muscle but have more skill dribbling the ball. They also might have more range on their shot so they can be useful offensively in more places on the court.

BECAUSE THE SMALL FORWARD AND SHOOTING GUARD PLAY NEAR THE SIDELINES, OR SIDES, OF THE COURT AND DO SIMILAR THINGS, THEY'RE OFTEN CALLED THE "WINGS" ON A COURT.

13

POWER PLAYERS

Power forwards are the "four" on a basketball team. They're usually the second-tallest and second-strongest player on the team. Power forwards need to do a few things very well. They must rebound well on offense and defense. Defensive rebounds are a big part of basketball because they limit the opposing team's chances to score.

Power forwards often must set screens to free up other players on offense. They also score points themselves, usually near the basket or in the space between the key and the three-point line. This is called a midrange shot. Power forwards with a good jump shot are very important!

SETTING SCREENS

Power forwards need to be good at setting screens. This is a play where the forward reaches a certain spot on the court and stops moving! A screen gets in the way of a defender that's chasing the player with the ball or lets a player with the ball run a certain play.

GETTING OFF A MIDRANGE JUMPER WHILE THE OTHER TEAM'S DEFENDERS ARE NEARBY IS A SPECIAL SKILL THAT MAKES POWER FORWARDS GREAT OFFENSIVE PLAYERS.

FRONT AND CENTER

The center is almost always the tallest player on the team. They take any **tip-offs** in a game. Centers in the National Basketball Association (NBA) are often 7 feet (2.1 m) tall or more! They play closest to the hoop, taking passes from the point guard and dribbling their way into the key. Most often, centers match up against other centers in a position known as the post.

In the post, centers try to make the defender back up to get close enough to the basket to dunk. They're great at getting high-percentage shots, which are shots close to the basket that are most likely to go in.

SHOT SELECTION

The dunk is just one kind of shot a center should be able to make. Playing in the post means they have to get creative, **banking** shots off a net's backboard and making space under the net between defenders to keep their shots from being blocked. Some can even make **hook shots** and short jump shots!

THE TWO TALLEST PLAYERS IN NBA HISTORY WERE CENTERS. MANUTE BOL AND GHEORGHE MURESAN WERE BOTH 7 FEET, 7 INCHES (2.3 M)!

OFF THE BENCH

One player who doesn't often get recognized enough on a basketball team starts the game on the bench. This is called the sixth player, because they're often the sixth player to enter the game for a team. This player can play different positions and can **replace** anyone on the court to give a team a different lineup or style on the floor.

This is where basketball gets **complicated**. Teams can substitute, or trade out, a big player and bring in another point guard to go "small." Teams could also go "big" by switching out a guard for another taller, stronger player like a power forward.

BETTER THAN THE STARTERS?

The first person off the bench in basketball often has some skills that make them better than the **starters** in certain ways. They may be more accurate shooters or better at defense. A basketball coach uses this player to give a boost to their team in one area while giving their starters a bit of rest on the bench.

PLAYING DEFENSE

Playing defense in basketball seems pretty simple. Players match up against their **opponents** in their positions and do their best to stop them from scoring points. Defending a player in basketball is called guarding them.

Guarding talented offensive players in basketball is hard! Defenders need to have quick **reflexes** in order to **react** to what a player does while dribbling. The best defensive players can guard another player one-on-one, or without help from their teammates. But teammates are there to help players if they need it. Teamwork is an important part of playing defense in basketball.

THE STOPPER

Some teams have a special bench player they keep just to play defense. This is called a "stopper." They may not have the best skills on offense, but they are usually the best defensive player on the team. When a team needs to stop the other team from scoring, the stopper checks into the game and guards the opposing team's star players.

PERSON OR ZONE

There are many different types of defense in basketball. Person-to-person defense is when every player is given an opposing player to guard at all times. In men's basketball games, this is called man-to-man defense. This kind of defense matches players based on their size and skill.

A zone defense gives players a certain area of the floor to guard. Offensive players move in and out of these zones trying to move defensive players and get chances to shoot. Zone defenses are named for where players are set up on the court. In a 2-3 zone, two players guard the frontcourt and three guard the backcourt.

Most defenses work best when they are given time to set up in the half court. Players get into position on their defensive side of the court and wait for the offensive team to attack the basket. Defenses can work further down the court, but the team on offense often has a better chance of finding ways through the defense when the defense stretches across the whole court.

SYRACUSE UNIVERSITY HEAD COACH JIM BOEHEIM HAS HIS ORANGE PLAY A 2-3 ZONE DEFENSE IN COLLEGE BASKETBALL.

PLAYING CLEAN

Fouls are called by officials when players make contact in a way that's against the rules. Bumping a player to the ground, hitting their hand while they dribble, and pushing someone out of your way are three ways you can foul someone. And if you're called for too many fouls, you can get kicked out of a game!

When a player is fouled trying to shoot, they get to shoot free throws. This is a free shot from the foul line worth one point. Good free-throw-shooting teams can score a lot of points this way.

OFFENSIVE FOULS

Not all fouls are called on defensive players. An offensive player can get a foul if they play too rough with defenders, too. If a defender has their feet set and they get bumped by a player with the ball, the offensive player will get called for charging! They get a foul and must turn the ball over to the other team.

DEFENDERS HAVE TO BE CAREFUL NOT TO TOUCH OTHER PLAYERS WHEN THEY TRY TO STEAL THE BALL. THEY'LL GET CALLED FOR A FOUL IF THEY MAKE CONTACT.

TWEENERS

Not all basketball players stay in one position forever. Some players just don't fit the usual positions on a basketball team and are moved from position to position throughout their time on the court. These players are called "tweeners" because they're "in between" positions.

Some hybrid, or mixed, positions in basketball include the point forward. A "swingman" is someone who can swing, or move, between the two and three—shooting guard and small forward—positions on the court. Tweeners can be important players that have many different talents. Coaches like players who can do a number of different things well on the court!

NOT GOOD ENOUGH

Not all tweeners are good at both positions they're stuck between. They may have certain skills that don't match the height or size of a player that usually plays that role on a team. Tweeners who don't have a set of skills that match the normal positions on a basketball team often don't stay in a team's lineup.

LEBRON JAMES IS AN EXAMPLE OF SOMEONE OFTEN THOUGHT OF AS A POINT FORWARD. HE'S BIG ENOUGH TO PLAY POWER FORWARD, BUT OFTEN RUNS THE OFFENSE FROM THE POINT!

SMALL BALL

Now that we've got some of the basic positions and rules of basketball down, let's try a bit of the harder stuff. When a team goes small, they often play a very fast lineup on the court. Teams that play "small ball" try to race past bigger teams on the fast break to score points before the bigger opposing players can defend them.

One tweener position perfect for small ball is the stretch four. This is a fast power forward who plays close to the basket, but can shoot accurately from behind the three-point arc. As the game changes, new sets of skills are needed for basketball players!

LISTEN UP

If you want to learn more about basketball, talk to some coaches. They know more about the game than anyone, and they're always trying to teach players how to get better. Whether it's about defensive positions or ways to make your shot better, a coach can help you learn more about the game.

COACHES WANT TO HELP YOU GET BETTER AND LEARN YOUR POSITION. THE BETTER YOU PLAY, THE BETTER THE TEAM PLAYS!

GLOSSARY

accurate: free from mistakes; able to hit the target

bank: to bounce

complicated: made of many different parts

design: to make a plan for something

dribble: to bounce without stopping

dunk: a basketball shot where a player jumps up and drops the ball through the net. Also, to make a basketball shot where a player jumps up and drops the ball through the net.

hook shot: a shot in basketball where a player uses one hand to throw the ball over their shoulder when they're facing away from the hoop

opponent: a member of the other team in a game

react: to act in answer to a situation or action

reflexes: the ability to react quickly

replace: to take a player's spot on the floor

starter: one of the first five players on the court for a basketball team

tip-off: the start of a play in basketball where the ball is thrown in the air between two opposing players

FOR MORE INFORMATION

BOOKS

Challen, Paul. *What Does a Small Forward Do?* New York, NY: PowerKids Press, 2016.

Graves, Will. *Make Me the Best Basketball Player.* Minneapolis, MN: SportsZone, 2017.

Yomtov, Nelson. *Being Your Best at Basketball.* New York, NY: Children's Press, 2017.

WEBSITES

Basketball Positions
jr.nba.com/basketball-positions/
Find out more about player positions in the NBA on its official site.

Player Positions
hooptactics.com/basketball-player-positions
Learn more about the basics of player positions here.

Types of Defenses
hooptactics.com/Basketball_Basics_Defenses
Get more information about the basics of playing defense here.

INDEX